The Fall and Rise

Sansika Uthayakumar

I dedicate these poems to my incredible family,
especially my mother and father, whose
unwavering support has been a constant
throughout my life and in the writing process. I
also dedicate these poems to all those who are
determined to find beauty in life despite the
struggles they may face.

Table of content

Part 1: The Inhibitions

They say art is best when you are broken,
Excuses for why we break ourselves
Over and over again.
But you stood there, like a masterpiece
Full of life and arrogance.
The kind of arrogance one loves,
But only a few understand.

Unbothered by the uncertainties and depths
Of life that drown the energy of an overthinker.
But you were so different.
You had so many reasons to be broken,

Yet still, you were a moving, living art.

Perhaps the art of forgiveness
Comes from the understanding
Of the complexities of
Flaws that strangle humankind,
Leading to behaviors
That rarely follow the
Footprints of the waves.

Perhaps the art of forgiveness
Comes from the longing
That, now, we can speak
To our actions and see
Our wrongdoings as
Little miscalculations,
Moments that make us stumble
And lose our posture,
But remind us that we are
Only human.

We hide behind the captures of
Casual conversations.
We are at war with the
Lingering informations of
Our potential.
How can we find the pathway
That crosses with our
Ambitions and insecurities,
And guide them both
Toward the peacemaking
Of the hindering
Potentials towards
Sacrificing thoughts
Of self - doubt.

And I hope that someday
Our fears will be tied so high,
That we never drown in
Self-doubt.
And that,
Our thoughts will rise above,
While we stay grounded.
And that today,
We'll understand
Yesterday's pain.

I was always a strong builder,
Constructing comments and criticisms
Like stone walls I could never
Climb my way through.
And I was a building
That learned to stand strong,
In the face of criticisms,
In the midst of storms,
That once pulled me apart.
I was hiding,
Yet standing forcefully.

Because sometimes,
There is more beauty in parallel lines
That refuses to interrupt each other's paths.
And sometimes,
There is more safety in distance,
For up close, we face each other's demons.
And in this place called life,
We are all artists rehearsing for our moment on
stage,
Where we can display all we've
Learned, and all we long to unlearn.

Lovers and haters
This is a gathering
Once and for all,
I've filled the vacancy
With melodies I composed myself.
This is just a warning
For the wrong lovers and haters
Before you enter,
Thinking there's space.

Her poetry
Her poetry stains souls,
Deeper than a soulful wound,
Taking up more space than
Existence ever could.
Her words are arrows,
Shooting at the faultiness of the world,
While cherishing the beauty
Within the unseen.

Children growing into adulthood,
While adults try to crawl
Back to days of innocence.
The struggle of life's long war with the present,
And the longing for the past,
Becomes a cycle
Living to the tunes of regret and remembrance.

Some days I am the rain,
Sprinkling moisture for growth.
Some days I am the accessories
You cover up with
Elegant, but empty.
Some days I am the storm,
Some days I am the
Quiet resolve.
And on days like this,
I am still trying to figure it out.

To write beautifully,
It must be difficult, they say
Open hearts that dance to melodies,
Constantly reopening to memories,
Smiling away the path to the finish line.
Welcoming sorrow and pain with water and smiles,
Leaving spaces for positivity to flow through,
Like bees stinging, swelling.
It is difficult, I say,
For writing happiness
Is making an ocean from drops.
For writing sorrow,
Your body is a compass,
And it's only direction is south.
To write beautifully,
It must be difficult.

Art is at its best
When you are broken.
Maybe that's why
You always find a way
To break yourself
Over and over again.

People are strange

So are you, and I.
You told me you liked my flaws
and my flawless strengths.
So I offered you my beating heart,
in my weakest days.

You saw the truth through my eyes,
and lies through my mouth
when I told you I was strong.
When you found the pathway
to my faultiness,
I became your strength,
and you, my weakness.

Soldiers and warriors of tomorrow,
Learn from the worriers of today.
Your echoes may be small,
But that doesn't diminish your value.
Your voice may be unheard,
But please don't stop.

Make thunders from rainbows,
They'll say,
"You are young."
Please don't hold back the truth.
They'll ask for proof,
But don't play hide and seek
With your presence.

We come from a society of womanhood,
Taught obedience as our mother tongue.
For me, safety was sewn into my body,
But I never knew if I should
Follow the crowd or stand alone,
In the darkest of times
Times when I, as a young girl,
Had never been taught the way to navigate.

So I hid, in my room,
Concealing poetry of power,
Under layers and layers of clothing
A quiet rebellion,
Waiting for the day to speak.

On days like this,
My body finds shelter in the bed,
And my soul, buried in a hole.
On days like this,
I can't think of poetry,
Or be a poem.

On days we feel like sinking boats,
Asking permission to flow,
Building a shelter beneath the trees,
Floating above the rising tides
Of clouded sensations and unwavering doubts.

We stand, lost in a million questions
Of everything that could be awe,
But still, we hope each morning,
We make a new movement
Towards the cycle of independence.

She is beautiful,
For she refuses to throw away
Her questions, her unanswered
Entanglements, for the comfort
Of fleeting circumstances.
She swallows her doubts
In the face of conversation.

She is beautiful,
But to them,
They think beauty lies in the
Deceiving nature of momentary egos,
In unexamined traumas that
Shape us without our knowing.

I kept peace as weapons,
Maintained a distance.
Sorting it out only bred misunderstandings.
Little did I realize,
Peace with others
Waged war within myself.

I used to write so powerfully,
When I was breaking.
But now, in the process of fixing,
I don't know if writing helps
Or hinders the healing.

Most times, I believe there is beauty in sinking
boats,
Which remind us that sinking and rising,
Like the cycle of life, show us what life is really
about.
It gives us air to breathe, then takes it away
In the blink of a second,
Leaving us gasping, craving what air feels like.
Next to me stands a canvas of art,
Empty of paint
For there is beauty in art created by empty vessels.
Some days, there is creativity in sorrow.
They belittle us, but they don't know,
That people like you and I may shrink to ashes,
But we rise like warning fire,
Alive and alarming.

Like darkness, I'll remind you
What it feels like to be both lost and found
In words of trust
And actions of mistrust.
I'll show you both darkness
And light,
With equal doses of confusion.

Because we are like dust particles,
each playing individual roles
on a stage that refuses to
compromise for any.
Each true to their own,
but in the quest for competition,
we forget that
true victory is not measured
by external standards.

It surpasses the confines of boxes,
and is instead handpicked
by mindful variation,
holding true to the uniqueness
of human nature.

How deep is one's ambition,
that it cuts through the
flurry of mindless thoughts,
clouds of fading miscalculations?
How deep is one's ambition,
that it forgets to surpass
the weight of overthinking?

Does it ever cross one's mind
that ambitions, too,
search for a place to call home
tossed around with each passing trial
of life?

Can ambition find a home
in you?

How do you fit
Wonder, hate, love,
Lust, fear, moon, and sun,
In a soul, all at once,
And nothing,
And feel everything,
When just one person appears?
I guess that's a human.

The fight between what to do
and what already is
seems conflicted, caught between
desires that exist without purpose.
There are futures and promises built
without the presence of the
present moment.

Hold me in the depths of our
momentary pain; for it will
lead us down a pathway to
our secrets and sorrows.
Can we delve into the
curiosity of peace,
and the beginning of our
beautiful journey into a world
of silent moments,
where we are caught between
glances and the inhibitions
of what we could be?

They will pin you to boards
with their understanding of community.
Tell you your words fall flat,
off-pitch tunes that can no longer proceed
into the gentle lullaby of hope.
They hide the warmth of your soul
and call it protection from the heat,
crushing your hope with
newsletters full of endless reminders
about what is "achievable."

But the best lullabies are heard
from a crying child in the warmth,
where the reflections may blur,
but you will feel the shine give clarity.
The reminders of reality are haunting,
but the endless confusion
lands you closer to the purpose
of self-creation.

For the sake of our sanity,
do we speak up for wrongdoings,
or sing lullabies to those who are dependent?
Do we get lost in the indulgence
of all the upcoming possibilities?

Where does one cross the line
between what already is
and what one can be?

Let this pass too,
for it brought thunders of wisdom
wrapped in packages of surprises.
Let this pass too,
for it taught us that
voices come in many forms,
but our messages vary
based on our grit.
Let this pass too,
for the universe
never ignores
a stubborn soul.

Is there a way to
fly back to the roots
of the endings
of uncertainty?
To cherish each passing moment,
for it holds
all that we ever needed.

The pathway to the tip
of every moment,
reminding us of the beauty
that lies in the voices
of humanity.

In the wake of our demons,
I've forgotten to tell you
your presence has given me
the strength of day
and the rest of the night.

Your playfulness taught me
that wings are made
from human smiles.

Your words have the
force of a dozen tornadoes,
crashing toward you
with unexpected, welcome waves.

Your affection reaches
the hidden scars,
promising a better day.

Can you always find a way
to stay near me?
Can we embrace like waves,
coming together at the
intersection of day and night?

Nothing can dim the light from within.
When I write,
I wish to hide behind metaphors
shadows that always leave a trace.

When I write,
I wish to apologize
to the doubts that undermine
my own strength.

When I write,
I wish to break through the barriers
of self-doubt,
and finally see my true capacity.

They will tell you
the crowd is your ladder,
glory seen in each step
that climbs higher.
But no one mentions the precision
and the resistance required
to climb,
with conflicting thoughts
always winning over the calm.

There's more to the race.
We learn to admire the falling leaves
and the melting snow,
because true beauty
lies in what ordinary eyes fail to see.

Part 2: The Yearnings

You are my mother tongue
and a foreign country.
You bring light at night,
take away my breath
with each exchange of memories.
We remind each other that
the confusion of intimacy
is born from the anonymous nature
of authenticity.

In the search for touch,
we become the artist,
yearning for the
songs of our heart
to become melodies
of one's soul.

Can fear, for one
split second,
surrender to the immense
joy and courage
of the moment,
where we lose touch with
our demons
and create paintings
with our senses?

In the face of uncertainty,
I look to you with open eyes,
hoping your words
might guide me toward
the pathway of righteousness.
Maybe then, we'll understand
the love in your thoughts,
as they take shape in words
that can be sculpted
into sculptures for the uncertain.

Living in the fierce flow of movement,
Can we pause?
In the blink of a posture,
Is there a barrier to
The routine of daily motion?

You hold close to my weakness because
You know the way to my soul.
Hold onto this moment forever,
Because you and I are like
Twinkling stars.

I see the twinkle in your eyes
When you watch the sunset and sunfall.
Let's caress this moment forever.
Hold me in your knowledge,
For we may not fear what's coming
Tomorrow.

When I talk to you, I forget
The shortcomings of today
And tomorrow.

She walks into the crowd
with the grace of a thousand steps.
She knows the path to her destination
consists of countless wings,
waiting to soar
across the vast expanse
of the night sky.

Can we fall in love the way
Romance refuses to speak?
Can we caress in such a way
That there are no rules to follow?
Can we hold each other
Close to the face of sacrifice?

How do I call a lover
Who's never been mine in the first place?
How do I call a lover
Whose name resonates like strings of a violin?
How do I call a lover
Who plays hide and seek with his eyes
Words and actions tangled at once?
What do I call you,
A lover or a hater?

Let's converse with the stars,
honor the handpicked roses
that bloom to the rhythm of our heartbeat.
Let's fly into the world
of unconstructed selves,
asking for nothing
but the presence of vulnerability.

I find myself longing for the past,
The present, and the future all at once.
I miss the joy in your laughter,
The tears, the hatred.
I miss the person I was meant to be,
The person you used to be,
I love the person you are now.
Memories I forget to feel
Caresses, love,
Return to me habitually,
Like an empty void I never knew existed.
And all the words spoken are stamped
Like a recurring dream.
Beautiful nightmare,
you come and go
like the fleeting movements of desire.
Teach me how to attract,
how to make arrogance
look like the most alluring thing
in the room.

I've spent every day
trying to write our yearnings
into words that capture
your glances of longing.
Because in this moment,
can we dance to the rhythms
of our untold intimacy?
Can we turn these cravings
into the long-awaited projects
of our hearts?
Hold me closer,
in the seconds of tension
that still keep us apart.

The true pathway to the heart of
love and the hands of sacrifice
is through the eyes of admiration.
Can I rewrite you as poetry,
for you are filled with
the possibilities of masterpieces,
combined with the precision
of a long-awaited verse.

Dear woman,
with the dearest of hearts,
hold on to your unwavering
strength of smile,
which dignifies into
different paths of direction
for all these girls
who seek the pathways
that lead them to their destinations
and teach them the power of faith.

The rhythms of our solitude
seek to find harmony between
untold desires and ambitions,
dangling from ropes
of tightly sewed words,
held back by our inhibitions.

The moments of each passing light
caress the silences of untold trials
and sleepless nights,
eyes filled with hopes of what we owe to be.
Little did the innocence of childhood
ever estimate the heights we would reach.
But sleep easy,
for tomorrow morning,
you are one step closer to
the person you will see in your reflection.

We will flow
in a state of charm.
Can you hold me
close to your arm,
always,
in this moment of chaos
let's celebrate our calm.

Each delay speaks to its reward.
What is lost today
comes back tomorrow,
in a form you might recognize
or in a way that surprises you.
But know this: each fall
awakens a rise
a rise that fights back,
an equal force with the audacity
to rise above the setback.

So do not fear the fall,
for it humbles you,
preparing you for the rise.

And in all the world, show me the way
To the ocean.
Let my house be drowned by the wave
That rose last night.
Your skin, like dawn and mine, like dust.
I want you to come to me, like the afternoon,
For I love you this way because I know no other
way.
What is stronger than the human heart,
That falls for you over and over,
Yet finds a way to protect you inside?
You are a dangerous collection of
All my favorite yearnings.

I am the sea,
My body is the breeze.
We are the wind, checking in
On the moments of flow,
Capturing patterns that
Connect us to the different paths
Of nature.
Our thoughts collide, like waves
Crashing together,
Waiting to be captured
By the never ending longings.

You are a hurricane wrapped in a bandage
soft enough to let yourself flow,
but strong enough to keep
the best parts of you hidden
from the world.

I let you go because
In our grip, there was
No longer the natural
Flow of unfiltered rhymes.
We were bound by the
Questions of safety,
When we forgot how
Freedom feels in love.
In the quest for long-term,
We disregarded our
Short-term desires that
Made us tear up at
The thought of
Endless possibilities.

Will there be a
Way back to the reunion
Of 'us' in this lifetime,
Where we forgive the
Children we were
And accept our childish
Desires, which carry us
Toward the long days?

Will our reunion
Speak to parts of our
Secrecy that we were
Unable to tame in one another?

Will our reunion
Still make us feel alive,
And bring us to our
Unsolved intimacies?

Hold me close to your
Flaws,
Let's tie a knot
To the secrets
And fly away
Into the depths of
Wavering questions,
And float in all
The answers.

Let's sprout in each other's
long-awaited togetherness,
one seed at a time.
Let's unravel the beauty
of each potential,
planting our minds
in each other's endless possibilities.
And sacrifice our wild temptations
for the growth of these ideas.

Because with you,
I want to experience
the world
hand in hand.

Is there a way to drown
In your skin, and
Collect the melanin,
Turning it into a
Dancing angel?
Your eyes, ones that
Compete with the
Sprouts of seeds
That refuse to stay
Hidden in the soil.
And your smile
Fights the devil,
Sprinkling you with
Unwavering
Glances.

She is a wave,
Softening the areas of drought
For the better,
Erasing the footprints of scars
All at once.
She is a mother.

My heart yearns for you
In all the places I've
Lost to time,
Searching for you in
The surface of mysteries
And in the depths of
Truth.
My heart yearns for you
In places I can only begin
To understand,
Surpassing the limits
Of words
That can ever be shared.

You are like the sounds
of my heartbeat
I fail to notice it,
recurring, replaying
in my memories.

But you are the only thing
I hear,
the only thing I feel,
when I want
and need to.

She is fearlessly imperfect,
Because in imperfection,
She finds her identity,
And loses it every time
She aims for perfection.

Out of all the things you are,
Your kindness shines with bravery,
You see love even while you're breaking,
And still, you love while you're healing
And in you, I find my home.

When we become
Each other's strength and weakness,
Knowing the pathways
To each other's fault lines,
But refusing to tear them open
And when we can look past
The uncertainty of tomorrow
And the weight of our flaws,
We will be forever.

Your smile speaks
To your innocence,
And you look at her
With quiet modesty.
Your words hold
Close to your character,
And your eyes
They tear apart pain
With a tenderness,
Like a longing mother.
In a world that fears identities,
Your masculinity is one
To be in awe of.

Can we sparkle our way
To living in a world that demands
Composure over creativity,
Structure over satisfaction?
When will we smile at our
Present pain and greet
It with open arms, knowing
It too, shall pass?
We're lost in the love
For direction,
But in the path we walk,
We find our way
Not defined by others,
But by the journey itself.

Hold me in your arms,
Let's kiss each other
In the wake of forever.
Will you keep our promises
As the day fades,
And the dawn awakens?
When we fly to the moon
And fall back to earth,
Let us hear the rawness
Of new beginnings.

Kiss my scars from today,
Make them fly back to me
When I forget my roots.
Will you keep my
Longings of days
And the shortness of breaths,
All born from the fear of
Tomorrow?

Can we kiss like
we've missed every
other chance,
in the wake of each night
and the fall of each morning?
Can we kiss like
we've missed every
other chance?

In the Depths of a Museum

They stood side by side,
viewing the intriguing complexities
beyond displayed art,
written songs,
and spoken poems.

There are more complexities,
more artistic articulations,
within the individuals,
for beyond the reach of a paint stroke,
beyond words sewn soothingly,
beyond any understanding.

The words may be mine,
the rhymes and the metaphors
that slip into beauty,
but the depths of darkness,
the measure of light,
are all yours.

He was a fighter.
She was a warrior.
They both loved the fight in them,
and caressed the flaws in them
with hands that knew
strength in every scar.
All at once,
they were in love.

You stood high,
A being full of life, arrogance, and confidence,
Teaching me the fragility within.
The strength in your glance
Lingers, a lifetime stored away
In the corners of desires.
Your confidence speaks in action,
And your actions capture souls,
Tucking them between the lands of daydreams
And winds that lift us to heights
We never thought we'd reach.

She carries light,
She carries darkness,
She carries the universe,
All at once.
She is called the MotherLand,
A force that balances light and dark
In the face of endless struggles.

Beautiful

A word so loosely tied together,
To sound like magic,
But there is so much tragedy
Behind the scenes.

You see the beauty
The way her eyes, like almonds, soften into raisins,
Her golden teeth widen for a smile full of grace.
But there is so much more,
So much more than beauty alone.

Why do you not see that part of her,
Where strength and vulnerability
converge into a rhythm of a never ending melody?

She is a wave,
Softening the areas of drought, bringing life
And erasing the footprints of scars
All at once.
She is a mother.

I want to hear a poem so beautiful
That it brings my childhood back, inch by inch,
Enough to stir the innocence
Stored deep within every child's heart.

I want to hear a poem so authentic
It makes you fall in love with the strange,
And stay curious, seeking all that life can offer
I want to hear a person so beautiful
That you, too, are the poem I've been longing for.

She paints words into harmony,
Creates music with silent breath,
And lays bare the strength in vulnerability.
The words may be hers,
But you are all the meaning.

I love your masculinity,
Masculine enough to shoot the
Look of a warrior.

I love your femininity,
Feminine enough to
Understand the depths of this
Worrier.

In your eyes,
I long to be seen.
In your touch,
I crave to be felt.
In your love,
I wish to drown,
And rise again, reborn.

For every moment of fall,
There shall be an equal rise.
For every moment of doubt,
There shall be immense courage.
For every moment of low,
There shall be an equal high.

Sometimes I feel like the ocean,
Erasing my own footprints,
Listening to the rhythms of our lost
melodies.
Is there a way back to the pathways
that take us flying back to
the true definitions of immeasurable
happiness?
Sometimes, words run deep into
the measurements of one's lost,
self-manipulated insecurities.
And moments of longing days
shall remind us that
one's worth is calculated in
the values of never-ending thoughts
which wander endlessly, like a
lover longing to feel you.

You make waters flow,
rivers wide open.
Your one look of confidence and arrogance
combines to create the
rhythm of multiple
orchestras, ordering their
obedience to your
sweet gestures.

Your glances win over
the shortcomings of
the ego left within
individuals.
You somehow always manage to
reach parts of her that
one could not
see with the naked eye.

Let's rebuild the secret of our bond.
I liked it better when the distance called for
answers
your silence wished for
moments of embrace.
The call for direction,
when all we wanted
was to wander
and be lost in the best possible way.

When I saw you,
Our eyes locked with each other,
creating a moment of longing
one that still longs to be.
Caught between your glares,
which slip into your lips,
holding the passage
into our moments of
intimacy.
You look as though your
features were made
with the precision of
a handcrafted masterpiece.
If only every artist
knew the key to such creation,
we would be in awe of
the human art piece.
Art like you is made
to be admired with
patience.

Let's lock hands, one finger at a time,
Unfold the mess of our fears.
Spend hours with the dust of nature,
Hide behind the lines of our untold dreams.
Can we pause our inhibitions
In a moment of wonder that only we are capable of?
Let's store it away in places of memory,
For when we need to remember
The void of touches.

In your words, I want to
build a place to rest.
Each reassurance you give
fills me with the hope of a lifetime.
Can I lay on your shoulders,
for they remind me that
the best pleasures
are found in the comfort of you
in the human version of your love.

The End